The Automobile Joke Book

The #1 Joke Book for All Car Enthusiasts and Petrolheads!

Hugh Phunnie

HUGH PHUNNIE

© Copyright 2022 Hugh Phunnie - All rights reserved.

The content contained within this book may not be reproduced, duplicated or transmitted without direct written permission from the author or the publisher.

Under no circumstances will any blame or legal responsibility be held against the publisher, or author, for any damages, reparation, or monetary loss due to the information contained within this book. Either directly or indirectly.

Legal Notice:

This book is copyright protected. This book is only for personal use. You cannot amend, distribute, sell, use, quote or paraphrase any part, or the content within this book, without the consent of the author or publisher.

Disclaimer Notice:

Please note the information contained within this document is for educational and entertainment purposes only. All effort has been executed to present accurate, up to date, and reliable, complete information. No warranties of any kind are declared or implied. Readers acknowledge that the author is not engaging in the rendering of legal, financial, medical or professional advice. The content within this book has been derived from various sources. Please consult a licensed professional before attempting any techniques outlined in this book.

By reading this document, the reader agrees that under no circumstances is the author responsible for any losses, direct or indirect, which are incurred as a result of the use of the information contained within this document, including, but not limited to, — errors, omissions, or inaccuracies.

HUGH PHUNNIE

SPECIAL BONUS!
WANT THIS BOOK FOR *FREE*?

Get *FREE*, unlimited access to it and all my new books by joining the Fan Base!

Scan with your camera to join!

HUGH PHUNNIE

THE AUTOMOBILE JOKE BOOK

The #1 Joke Book for All Car Enthusiasts and Petrolheads!

HUGH PHUNNIE

TABLE OF CONTENTS

Dad Jokes 11

At the Racetracks 31

The Infamous Lada 39

Electric Cars 57

American Cars 67

Asian Cars 83

European Cars 95

Long Jokes 111

Dad Jokes

HUGH PHUNNIE

1.

Kids in the backseat cause accidents.

Accidents in the back seats cause kids.

2.

I have been to a car show all weekend.

I'm exhausted.

3.

A man is washing his car with his son.

The son asks, "Dad, can't you just use a sponge?"

4.

What happens when Kermit the Frog's car breaks down?

It gets toad.

5.

Why is Miss Piggy such a bad driver?

Because all she does is hog the road!

6.

What's a 10-letter word that starts with g-a-s?

Automobile.

7.

What do you get if your car is on fire?

Hot wheels!

8.

What do you call an underwater car?

A Scubaru.

9.

Where does a dog park its car?

In the barking lot.

10.

Why do chicken coops have only two doors?

If they had four, they would be chicken sedans.

11.

What kind of car does a snake drive?

An Ana-Honda!

12.

Why can't you walk behind a car?

Because you'll get exhausted.

13.

What is an autobiography?

An automobile's story.

14.

If you break the speed limit, can you fix it?

15.

What do you call a country that drives only rose-colored cars?

A "red carnation!"

16.

What kind of cars do cooks drive?

Chef-rolets!

17.

What do rodents power their cars with?

Weasel-diesel!

18.

"It takes thousands of bolts to put a car together, but only one nut to wreck it."

19.

Who can drive all their customers away and still make money?

Taxi drivers!

20.

What's a car's favorite meal?

Brake-fast.

21.

What do you get when you crash a cement truck into a bus full of convicts?

A bunch of hardened criminals.

22.

Knock, knock.

Who's there?

Cargo.

Cargo, who?

No, cargo beep-beep!

23.

"A car just ran over my foot," said James tiredly.

24.

"Fix that tire," said James flatly.

25.

What is a ghost's favorite car?

A Boo-gatti.

26.

What do you get when you cross a Mustang and an elephant?

A convertible with a giant trunk!

27.

What was the first car Henry Fordasaurus invented?

A Model T-Rex.

28.

One night I dreamed I was a muffler.

I woke up exhausted.

29.

What kind of vegetable do you need when you have a flat tire?

A-spare-agus!

30.

A man was driving his vehicle when he came across two paths.

Then one of his tires went flat. He came to a fork in the road.

31.

I couldn't work out how to fasten my seatbelt.

Then it clicked.

32.

What is the last thing that goes through a bug's mind before it hits the windshield?

Its butt.

33.

A truck carrying Vicks VapoRub overturned on the highway.

Amazingly there was no congestion for 8 hours straight.

34.

My daughter said I could never make a car out of spaghetti.

You should have seen the look on her face when I drove pasta.

35.

The next Bond should be a woman!

Can you imagine? Crazy car scenes with spectacular crashes, explosions, and all of that while she's parking?

36.

When is a vehicle not a vehicle?

Once it turns into a driveway.

37.

When Jimi Hendrix was 16, he was in a car crash.

Luckily it was just a Fender bender.

38.

Why did the washing machine schedule a test drive?

Because he wanted to go for a spin.

39.

Did you know all cars have snakes?

They're called windshield vipers.

40.

Why did the snail paint a big "S" on his car's hood?

Because he wanted people to shout, "Look at that S-car go!" when he drove past.

41.

Two French cheese trucks just crashed!

Looks like there's da' brie everywhere.

42.

I really need to get my car fixed.

What body shop to you wreck-amend?

43.

When I was a kid, your Uncle Fred used to put me in a tire and roll me down a hill.

Ah, those were the Goodyears.

44.

What's worse than raining cats and dogs?

Hailing taxis.

45.

Did you hear the University of Phoenix offers a program for used car salespeople?

Now you can major in car-deal-ology.

46.

You know what really grinds my gears?

Clutch failure!

47.

What's got four wheels and flies?

A garbage truck.

48.

What did the traffic light say to the car?

"Turn your head while I'm changing!"

49.

You should get a job at a transmission repair shop.

I'm sure you'll get used to the early-morning shifts.

50.

What kind of vehicle does a skeleton drive?

A Zam-bone-i.

HUGH PHUNNIE

At the Racetracks

51.

A janitor gets accepted into NASCAR.

His car goes "Broom, Broom"

52.

How do you watch NASCAR without a TV?

You flush a bag of M&M's down the toilet.

53.

Did you hear the one about the F1 race drive that got into an accident?

He broke almost every single bone in his body and the doctors told him he would never drive again.

He was absolutely shattered.

54.

NASCAR is officially cancelled after discovering it's just a human traffic ring.

55.

Why doesn't NASCAR have an Internet Explorer car?

Because it would keep crashing.

56.

Why was Harry Potter surprised when Ferrari won the Formula One race?

Because he Expecto'd Petronas.

57.

What does NASCAR stand for?

Non-Athletic Sports Cantered Around Rednecks.

58.

Why does Ben Shapiro hate NASCAR?

Because the cars only turn left.

59.

WHAT DO WE WANT?

RACECAR NOISES!!!

WHEN DO WE WANT IT?

NNNEEEEEEOOOOOOOOOWWWWWWWW!!!!!

60.

Why don't race car drivers eat before a race?

So they don't get Indy-gestion.

61.

Why are race car drivers the best people to go to for dating advice?

They're trained to look for red flags.

62.

Who was that Austrian F1 driver, Niki?

Lauda?

WHO WAS THAT AUSTRIAN F1 DRIVER?

63.

What do you do for a living?

I race cars.

Wow! Do you win a lot of races?

No. The cars are usually much faster.

64.

If I love Formula 1 and hate NASCAR, does that make me a race-ist?

65.

What do you get when you cross a race car with a spud?

Crashed potatoes.

HUGH PHUNNIE

The Infamous Lada

HUGH PHUNNIE

66.

Why doesn't Lada compete in Formula 1?

No need for rushin' when you're Russian.

67.

How do you double the value of a Lada?

You fill up its tank.

68.

How do you make a Lada depreciate in half of its value?

You break off the antenna.

69.

What happens when you scratch off the paint of a luxurious Lada?

You read "Heineken" on the squashed and recycled beer cans.

70.

Why does a Lada have an electric rear windshield?

It's for warming your hands when you're pushing it.

71.

What do you call a Lada-owner who says that he has gotten a speeding ticket?

A dreamer.

72.

What's the difference between a Lada and a condom?

There's iron in a condom.

73.

What do you call a Lada on the top of a hill?

A miracle.

74.

What do you call two Ladas on the top of a hill?

A mirage.

75.

What do you call it when there are several Ladas on the top of a hill?

A junkyard.

76.

How do you overhaul a Lada?

You run.

77.

What's the difference between having a Lada and having the flu?

You can get rid of the flu.

78.

What do you call a Lada with a long antenna?

A bumper car.

79.

What's the difference between a regular model of a Lada and the sports edition?

There are a pair of sneakers in the trunk of the sports edition.

80.

Why don't Ladas have sunroofs?

So you don't mistake it for a recycling bin.

81.

How do you get a Lada to run twice as fast?

You buy an extra hamster.

82.

How do you make a police officer laugh?

You tell him that your Lada has been stolen.

83.

How do you make your Lada sportier?

You wear a pair of Adidas when driving.

84.

What can you read from page four to page 143 on a Ladas instructions manual?

Train and bus schedules.

85.

What is the instructions manual called?

Mein Kampf.

86.

What's the difference between a Lada and a Jehovah's witness?

You can shut the door on a Jehovah's witness.

87.

What do you call a Lada with two exhaust pipes?

A wheelbarrow.

88.

How do you best avoid speeding tickets?

You buy a Lada.

89.

What's a Lada owners second biggest wish?

To get a speeding ticket.

90.

What's the highest wish for a Lada owner?

To have a real car.

91.

How do you fit 10 Lada-owners on the backseat of a car?

You throw a penny on the backseat.

92.

Where can you find the smallest piece of a Lada?

Between the ears of its owner.

93.

When does a Lada have its highest speed?

On the assembly line.

94.

How do you make a Lada go from 0 to 60 mph?

You push it off a cliff.

95.

What do you call a Lada with safety belts?

A backpack.

96.

Have you ever thought of why you always get a dog with the purchase when you buy a brand-new Lada?

It's with the prize so you have company when you're walking home.

97.

How do you make a Lada go faster?

You put on another rubber band.

98.

How do you make a Lada disappear?

Rust remover.

99.

How many factory workers does it take to build a Lada?

Two. One who cuts and one who glues.

100.

What's in a first aid kit of a Lada?

A straitjacket.

101.

What do you get if you cross a turtle and a hedgehog?

A Lada with studded tires.

102.

What do you call a Lada with a seat and a functioning steering wheel?

Progress.

103.

How long does it take to disassemble a Lada?

Two minutes. You set it to idle, then it does the rest itself.

104.

Did you know that Lada is the world's most powerful car?

It can pull a line all the way from Seattle to Atlanta.

105.

Why does a Lada have rear window wipers?

For removing the flies that smack into it.

106.

What is the difference between a Lada and a tampon?

A tampon comes with its own tow rope.

107.

What's the difference between a Lada and the principal's office?

It's less embarrassing if your friends see you leaving the principal's office.

108.

How can you improve a Lada?

Put a Dacia engine in it.

109.

When does the Lada owner sit with a hose from the Lada's exhaust pipe to his mouth?

When he needs to give it artificial respiration.

Electric Cars

HUGH PHUNNIE

110.

New Tesla's don't come with a new car smell, they come with an Elon Musk.

111.

Why did it take up until last year for Volkswagen to finally manufacture electric cars in the United States?

Because it took them awhile to get the bugs worked out.

112.

What did Bruce Wayne say to Elon Musk?

With great power comes great electricity bill.

113.

What do the Germans call a Tesla?

A Volts-wagon.

114.

Chevrolet is about to introduce another fully electric car.

Many people think it's great, but others think it's just re-Volting.

115.

What do you call a criminal driving a Tesla?

A Joule Thief.

116.

My friend told me the range of his Tesla and I was like Watt!

117.

Who solved the mystery of the stolen Tesla?

Sherlock Ohms.

118.

Someone hit me with their Tesla and now my Head Hertz.

119.

If you're driving a Tesla and it gets stolen, is it now called an Edison?

120.

Did you hear about the Tesla owner in jail?

He was charged with battery.

121.

If Dodge made an electric car, would it be called a Dodge Chargeable?

122.

According to a new poll 91 percent of people are dissatisfied with their cars.

The other 9 percent are Tesla owners.

123.

You want a man that drives a Tesla, but your dad drives a Toyota.

Why can't you be humble like your mom?

124.

What did the German boy say after pushing his brother out of a Tesla?

Look Mom, No Hans.

125.

What does the speedometer say on the BMW i3 when you put it in reverse?

"GAME OVER"

126.

Did you know it's against the law to own an electric vehicle in Africa?

They only allow Mada-Gas-Cars.

127.

I wanted to buy a new electric car.

Their prices are just too shocking.

128.

An electric car hit a cyclist the other day.

It got arrested for assault with a battery.

129.

Rumor has it that Dyson is going to develop an electric car by 2030.

I bet it'll really suck.

HUGH PHUNNIE

American Cars

130.

I found a very nice 1967 Camaro. The paint was clean, it started beautifully. When I opened the door there was a disgusting dead cat on the floor.

I was ready to walk away from the deal, but the owner agreed to replace the carpet.

131.

Two Cadillac drivers got in a fender-bender, got out of their cars, and then started yelling at each other. Within a few seconds they were in a fistfight.

I guess you could say things Escaladed quickly.

132.

What do you say to a young woman driving a Buick?

Sorry about your grandmother.

133.

General Motors will introduce two new warning lights for their cars!

One to tell you that you need a new engine and the other to tell you that you need a new car.

134.

If you want to be a General Motors engineer, your memory needs to be perfect.

You have to recall everything.

135.

Americans have General Motors.

Russians have General Winter.

136.

What do you call a domesticated Chevrolet?

A tame impala.

137.

I just replaced a bunch of parts on my Chevy muscle car and made it a Pontiac muscle car.

Now it's a trans Trans-Am.

138.

What do Fort McMurray and a 1998 Pontiac Sunfire have in common?

Both are full of white trash and smell like burning oil.

139.

There was a bad accident at the Air Force base.

A jeep ran over a bag of popcorn and killed two kernels.

140.

My sex life is like a Pontiac.

I usually find it on the side of the road.

141.

What do Ford Mustangs and horny people have in common?

They both create accidents willingly.

142.

It's crazy how much people love Ford Mustangs.

I hear they're a real hit with the crowd.

143.

Hear about the Cadillac-worshipping Satanist?

He sold his soul to the Deville.

144.

I finally bought something today that I've wanted since 1998.

A 1998 Cadillac.

145.

Chrysler is introducing a new car to its line-up to honor Donald Trump.

The Dodge Drafter will go into production in Canada this year.

146.

Did you hear about the Dutch painter that swapped a Hemi into his Chrysler Voyager?

Everyone in town said, "Look at Vincent's van go!"

147.

What would Chrysler's version of the Ford Focus be called?

Chrysler Concentrate.

148.

The Dodge Ram has always confused me.

I mean, which do you want to do? Dodge it or Ram it?

149.

What do you call a Dodge made out of silicon?

A Hemi-conductor!

150.

A Chevy Silverado, a GMC Sierra, a Ford F150, a RAM 1500, and a Toyota Tacoma are driving in convoy.

Best pickup line ever.

151.

What's the best kind of car to use in a demolition derby?

Dodge.

152.

Why did Chevrolet put a cross as their emblem?

So you can pray to God the car starts.

153.

Why is Pokémon Go a lifesaver?

Because it gives Chevy owners something to do while they walk home.

154.

What did the Ford say to the Buick on the side of the road?

Rust-in-peace.

155.

Why do Chevys have magnetized bumpers?

So they can pick up other Chevys parts while driving.

156.

What do GMC Truck owners and a bottle of beer have in common?

They're both empty from the neck up.

157.

Why did the cat sleep under the Chevy?

Because he wanted to wake up oily.

158.

Why did the Chevy cross the road?

To pick up the bits it lost yesterday.

159.

Why does the new Ford Escape parallel park itself?

Because white trash can only trailer park!

160.

What should the Ford Mustang really be called?

The Ford Rustang.

161.

Do you know what GM stands for?

General Maintenance.

162.

Do you know what FORD stands for?

Failure On Research & Development.

163.

Kids, I bought the cat a new car.

It's a Cat-illac.

164.

What type of car does the dog hate?

A Cor-Vet.

165.

My friend Marty owned a DeLorean.

He drove it from time to time.

166.

What happens when you leave your ADHD medication in your Ford Fiesta?

It turns into a Ford Focus.

Asian Cars

HUGH PHUNNIE

167.

What kind of car did Whitney Houston drive?

Hyundaiiiiiiiiiiiiiiiiiiiiiiii.

168.

My Muslim neighbors were fighting over their Suzuki and Nissan cars.

The Ciaz vs Sunny problems are getting out of hand.

169.

Whenever I get into my friend's car, I find him difficult to understand.

He starts speaking in a Hyundai Accent.

170.

My Toyota died today.

I think it was the Corollavirus.

171.

I recently got into an accident by over steering into a Korean car.

It could have been avoided if I had better Hyundai coordination.

172.

Did you know 60% of all Asian men have Cataracts?

The other 40% drive Mitsubishis.

173.

Can a Toyota stretch?

No, but a Mercedes-Benz.

174.

Want to hear a Nissan joke?

Nissan Juke.

175.

What kind of car is the same frontward and backward?

A Toyota.

176.

All the members of the Beatles drove Volkswagens, except for Paul McCartney, he drove a Bluebird.

177.

Want to hear a slow joke?

Toyota Yaris on the highway.

178.

Want to hear a long and a slow joke?

Traffic jams caused by the old Toyota Yaris driver.

179.

What do you call a Nissan that is styled and tuned for drifting?

A robot vacuum cleaner.

180.

What is a fast Honda like coming out of the closet?

You surprise everyone at first, but in the end your still gay.

181.

Almost all Mazda's are hybrid cars.

They burn both gas and engine oil.

182.

What do you call it when two Nissan Cubes get into an accident?

A wreck-tangle.

183.

All Hondas are rust guaranteed.

It's guaranteed that they will rust.

184.

Why was Buzz Lightyear at the Lexus dealership?

To go beyond Infiniti.

185.

A guy walks into my parts store and says he needs a gas cap for a KIA.

Sounds like a fair trade.

186.

They say Norio Suzuki died in an avalanche while searching for the yeti.

But think about it for even a little bit, you'll realize this so-called avalanche is really just a massive cover-up.

187.

What is Darth Vader's favorite Nissan vehicle?

The Rogue one.

188.

What kind of car does a Jedi drive?

A Toy Yoda.

189.

Do you know the similarity between any styled Asian car and a vacuum cleaner?

Both suck and look like something made for the Fast and the Furious franchise.

190.

Do you know what KIA stands for?

Korean Industrial Accident.

191.

Do you know what TOYOTA stands for?

The One You Oughta Tow Away.

192.

Do you know what SUBARU stands for?

Souped Up Broke Ass Racing Unit.

193.

Do you know what Honda stands for?

Honda Options: No Deal Available!

194.

Who is Kia's main competitor?

Nokia.

European Cars

195.

What's the difference between a Fiat and a golf ball?

You can drive a golf ball more than 200 yards.

196.

What's the difference between a Ferrari and six trash bags full of recyclable cans?

I don't have a Ferrari in my garage.

197.

How does a German cowboy say hello?

Audi.

198.

I went to a car dealership last week and saw a Lamborghini that really caught my eye.

I'm just waiting for my paycheck now so I can pay for an Uber and go see it again.

199.

Did you hear about the guy who was killed by an Aston Martin?

He got vanquished.

200.

What's even more difficult than getting your pregnant wife into a MINI Cooper?

Getting your wife pregnant in a MINI Cooper.

201.

What do you call an Indian in a Lamborghini?

Curry in a hurry.

202.

Did you hear that Fiat and Skoda have merged into a new car brand?

It's called Fiasko.

203.

Real Porsches are from the Porscheaux region of France.

Otherwise, they're just sparkling Volkswagens.

204.

Want to hear a long joke?

Volvo 960 Limo.

205.

What's the best part of Audi's customer service?

They answer within four rings.

206.

What language do Porsche drivers speak?

Porschuguese.

207.

What's the difference between a BMW and an elephant?

Elephants have a trunk up front and asshole in the back.

208.

How many BMW drivers does it take to screw in a lightbulb?

Doesn't matter, they won't use their blinker anyways.

209.

If you ever feel like your job has no purpose, always remember that right now, there is someone who is installing a turn signal in a BMW.

210.

If you ever feel like your job is meaningless, then remember that someone has the job of crash testing Volvos.

211.

Where do Volkswagens go when they retire?

The Old Volks Home.

212.

I put Truck Nuts on my fleet of Volkswagen Beetles.

Now I have genital Herbies.

213.

So a Volkswagen Beetle meets a tank.

Tank: What moron designed you? Your heart is in your ass!

Beetle: Look who's talking, dickhead!

214.

I wanted to buy an Audi.

But I can't A4'd it.

215.

What do Porsche and Apple have in common?

New product, same design.

216.

My neighbor recently bought a BMW, a Volkswagen, 2 Skoda's, a Mercedes and an Alfa Romeo.

I think he's got the car-owners virus.

217.

You know why Volkswagen cars are better?

They always come with one more light.

218.

What do Volkswagen and a boy going through puberty have in common?

They both lie about their emissions.

219.

Why does Master Yoda and the other Jedis prefer driving a Volkswagen?

Because the force is strong with T1.

220.

What do you get when you cross the Pope with a Lamborghini?

A Jedi. Force equals mass times acceleration.

221.

I bought a used Volvo from Neil Diamond on an online auto trader.

It's called Swede Car Online.

222.

What do you call an Audi that was in a head on collision?

An innie.

223.

If you had to choose between a long-lasting relationship and 10 million dollars what color would your Porsche be?

224.

Why did the Audi driver wave when he was let in?

Because he wasn't driving a BMW.

225.

As I understand it the Audi car company is opening a new factory in Texas to produce a new SUV to be called the Audi Neighbor.

226.

Who wins in a race between a Porsche and a Lamborghini?

Volkswagen.

227.

People get impressed when I tell them my home is designed by a famous Italian.

Until I invite them home and they realize I live in a Fiat.

228.

Want to hear a car joke?

BMW 2 Series.

229.

Do you know what VW stands for?

Very Worrisome!

230.

Do you know what FIAT stands for?

Failure in Automotive Technology.

231.

Do you know what VOLVO stands for?

Very Odd-Looking Vehicular Object.

232.

Do you know what SAAB stands for?

Sorry, Automobile Assembled Backwards.

HUGH PHUNNIE

Long Jokes

HUGH PHUNNIE

233.

Three automobile managers are at the urinal.

The first goes to the sink and dries his hands with so many paper towels that not even the smallest droplet remains. "At Opel, we learn to be extremely thorough," he says.

The second uses only one towel for this and remarks: "At BMW, we also learn to be extremely efficient."

The third walks past the sink and says, "At Daimler, we don't piss over our hands!"

234.

Two prostitutes were talking about clients when one of them points to the Mercedes across the street.

You see that car, the car owner afforded it because of me, said the first one with a smile on her face.

You know, that's not how it works, we don't give them money, they give it to us, the second said confused.

Yeah, I know, before he met me, he had the money to buy a Ferrari.

235.

A Boy Scout went around his neighborhood looking for a job.

"I'll pay you $20 to paint my porch," said one neighbor. The Scout agreed and went to work.

A few hours later, the Scout knocked on the neighbor's door and said, "I'm all finished, but your car is a Ferrari, not a Porsche."

236.

A police officer stops a car going 75 when the speed limit is 65. The officer asks the man driving if he realizes he was speeding.

The man replies, "Look right there - that sign says the speed limit is 75."

The officer explains that that's the highway number, not the speed limit. As he says this, he looks in the back of the car and sees an elderly woman breathing very heavily.

The officer asks her, "Are you okay?", to which she replies, "Yes, we just got off Highway 155".

237.

A Frenchman, a German, and a Russian are arguing about cars.

The Frenchman says: We use the Renault for travel inside our country, and the Peugeot when we travel outside the border.

The German says: Ach, ja! We do that too! We use the Volkswagen for travel inside our country, and the Mercedes when we go to foreign countries.

The Russian then says: Well, we do something similar, we use Ladas for travelling inside the motherland, and tanks everywhere else.

238.

"How can you watch Victoria's Secret Fashion Week but still claim you love only me?" My wife asked.

"The same way I watch Formula One the whole weekend but still drive my trusted 2012 Toyota Camry every day," I replied.

That satisfied her.

I just failed to mention that I take a rental at Enterprise when I go on business trips.

239.

Jesus drove a Honda, but never talked about it.

"For I did not speak of my own Accord" – John 12:49.

His old man had a Plymouth.

He drove Adam and Eve out of the Garden in a Fury.

Of all the trials of Job, the worst was the Pontiac "for he breaketh me with a Tempest, and multiplieth my wounds without cause" – Job 9:17

240.

Jamie the Jewish man died in a horrible car crash and his wife Ida rang the newspaper to put out his obituary.

It's $10 per word, said the man at the newspaper.

In that case, please put "Jamie died", she said.

Unfortunately, it's a minimum of 5 words, he replied.

Okay then, she said, please put "Jamie died. Volvo for sale."

241.

My uncle in Detroit tried to make a new kind of car. He took the engine from a Ford, the transmission of an Oldsmobile, the tires from a Cadillac, and the exhaust system from a Plymouth.

Really? What did he get?

Fifteen years.

242.

During the days of the Soviet Union a man walks into the local Lada dealership. He tells the salesman what color he wants and pays the full cost of the car.

The salesman takes the money and says he should come back to pick up the car in seven years.

Would that be in the morning or the afternoon? Asks the man.

What difference does it make? asks the salesman.

The man looks at the salesman and says: The plumber is scheduled to fix my toilet in the morning.

243.

An old man is in his Volvo driving home from work when his wife rings him on his cellphone.

"Honey," she says worryingly, "are you okay? Are you safe? I just saw in the news that there is a lunatic driving in full speed down the wrong side of the freeway."

"One?" he replied, "There are HUNDREDS of them!"

244.

What would you call Spiderman if he was a Greek who was into free running, had a debilitating disease and was backing up two cars?

Pita Parkour Parker with Parkinson's parallel parking a Pontiac pulling a pickup truck.

What would you call Spider-man if he was a Greek who was into free running, had a debilitating disease and was backing up two cars, while making rice?

Uncle Ben.

245.

A Texas rancher was visiting a farmer in Israel. The proud Israeli showed him around. "Here is where I grow tomatoes, cucumbers, and squash. Over there I built a play set for my kids, next to the doghouse," the farmer said.

The land was tiny, and the Texan was surprised by its small size. "Is this all your land?" he asked.

"Yes," the Israeli said proudly. "This is all mine!"

"You mean this is it? This is all of it?" the Texan said incredulously.

"Yes, yes, this is really all mine!"

"Well, son," said the Texan, "back home I'd get in my car before the sun'd come up and I'd drive and drive and drive, and when the sun set, why, I'd only be halfway across my land!"

"Oh, yes," replied the Israeli farmer wistfully, "I also used to drive a Skoda."

246.

A penguin is driving along the highway, when suddenly his engine starts running rough and he sees smoke in his rear-view mirror.

He pulls off the highway and finds the nearest service station and pulls up to the garage with the car shaking and sputtering. He tells the mechanic what happened, and the mechanic says, "Okay, give me 10 minutes to check it out."

Meanwhile, the penguin sees an ice cream shop across the street. Thinking this is a perfect time for a tasty treat, he heads over and gets himself an ice cream cone.

After he finishes, he walks back over to the garage, and asks the mechanic, "So did you find out what's wrong?"

The mechanic looks at the penguin and says, "it looks like you blew a seal."

The penguin quickly wipes his face and says, "Oh, no, that's just the ice cream."

247.

A banjo asked a fiddle to marry him. "Don't fret," he said. "Just duet and we'll live in harmony until the end of time."

Ten months later, the fiddle started to tip the scales. Her belly was noticeably bowed and before you could say concerto, out popped a minor.

Daddy banjo went to the Hyundai dealer and traded in his old Accent for a brand-new Sonata. After just a month, mama fiddle lost her keys at the bar and had a breakdown when she couldn't find it.

Apparently, it really struck a chord with daddy banjo because for the first time ever, he took a harsh tone with mama fiddle. He drove her home, lost his tempo, strung her up by the neck, and beat her.

Domestic violins!

248.

Toyota and Ford decided to do a rowing competition. They both got their best teams together and had them compete. The result was a disaster for Ford. The Toyota rowing team beat them by leagues.

Ford had a crisis meeting, hired the best analysts and consultants, and after half a year they came up with a conclusion: The Toyota rowing boat had 8 rowers and one cox while at Ford, one man was rowing and 8 yelled at him.

Ford's conclusion: The rower has to work harder.

Next year at the competition, Toyota won by an even larger margin.

So Ford had the rower fired.

249.

A woman breaks down in her VW Beetle. She stops at the side of the road and doesn't know what to do. She has no phone signal and doesn't see any cars or people in the area, so she feels stranded.

20 minutes go by and suddenly she sees a car in the far distance. He approaches but doesn't stop and neither does the next one. She is distraught.

She waits and waits when suddenly she again sees a car in the distance – this time a familiar one – a VW Beetle.

The driver stops next to her, and a man gets out: "I couldn't leave a fellow Volkswagen driver stranded out here! Let me help you and see what I can do"

He goes over to her car, checks it out, pops open the hood and says: "ah! I see the problem! You're missing the engine!"

"Oh no!" the woman exclaims, highly surprised, thinking how she could have lost it. The road was bumpy, perhaps that is why.

"You're in luck though," says the man, "I have a spare engine in my trunk!"

250.

In 1998 Enzo Anselmo Ferrari, after living a full life, died. When he got to heaven God was showing him around. They came to a modest little house with a small Ferrari flag in the window.

This house is yours for eternity, Enzo, said God, and continued: This is very special; not everyone gets a house up here.

Enzo felt special, indeed, and walked up to his house. On his way to the porch, he noticed another house just around the corner. It was a huge mansion with a carbon fiber sidewalk, a 50 feet tall flagpole with an enormous Porsche flag and in every window, a Porsche crest.

Enzo looked at God and said: God, I'm not trying to be ungrateful, but I have a question. Throughout my life I have been a good manufacturer; my cars won Le Mans and Formula One championships. Why does Ferdinand Porsche get at better house than me?

God chuckled and said, Enzo, that's not Ferdinand's house, it's mine!

251.

A man recently bought himself a new Dacia, but after a couple of days he's back at the dealership complaining about the performance.

The salesman who sold him the car asks him about the specifics.

Come outside, said the man, and I'll show you what I mean. So they go outside and the man points to a hill just further down the road.

You see that hill there? Asked the man, every time I go up there, I can't get past 40.

The salesman looks at the hill, and shrugs. You know, it's a pretty steep incline. For a Dacia, 40 really isn't that bad so I don't really see the problem.

The problem is that I live at 46.

252.

There was a Japanese man who went to America for sightseeing. On the last day, he hailed a cab and told the driver to drive to the airport. During the journey, a Honda drove past the taxi. Thereupon, the man leaned out of the window excitedly and yelled, "Honda, very fast! Made in Japan!"

After a while, a Toyota sped past the taxi. Again, the Japanese man leaned out of the window and yelled, "Toyota, very fast! Made in Japan!"

And then a Mitsubishi sped past the taxi. For the third time, the Japanese leaned out of the window and yelled, "Mitsubishi, very fast! Made in Japan!"

The driver was a little angry, but he kept quiet. And this went on for quite a number of cars.

Finally, the taxi came to the airport. The fare was US$300. The Japanese exclaimed, "Wah... so expensive!"

There upon, the driver yelled back, "Meter, very fast! Made in Japan!"

253.

A lawyer opened the door of his Tesla, when suddenly a car came along and hit the door, ripping it off completely. When the police arrived at the scene, the lawyer was complaining bitterly about the damage to his new precious electric luxury car.

"Officer, look what they've done to my Model S!", he said whiningly.

"You lawyers are so materialistic, you make me sick!!!" reported the officer, "You're so worried about your stupid Tesla, that you didn't even notice that your left arm was ripped off!"

"Oh my god," replied the lawyer, finally noticing the bloody left shoulder where his arm once was, "Where's my Rolex?"

254.

This guy had just bought a BMW M5 and decided to take it out and open it up. He was cruising along Dutch roads just admiring the beautiful scenery.

He decided to see how it ran at speed, so he took it up to 110kph. It felt great. Then up to 145kph. Then he saw the flashing lights in his rearview mirror. He decided to try to outrun the cop.

After a few minutes over 240kph he decided that this wasn't the smartest thing he ever did and pulled over. The cop came up, took his license without a word, looked it over. Then he said, "It's Friday, it's late. If you can give me an excuse for your behavior that I've never heard before, I'll let you off."

The guy thought a few seconds and said, "Last week my wife ran off with a cop and I was afraid you were trying to bring her back."

"Have a nice weekend," said the officer.

256.

A car mechanic was removing a cylinder-head from the motor of a Cadillac when he spotted a well-known cardiologist in his shop.

The cardiologist was there waiting for the service manager to come and take a look at his car when the mechanic shouted across the garage, "Hey Doc, want to take a look at this?" The cardiologist, a bit surprised, walked over to where the mechanic was working on the engine.

The mechanic straightened up, wiped his hands on a rag and asked, "So Doc, look at this engine. I will open its heart, take the valves out, repair any damage, and then put them back in, and when I'm finished, it works just like new. So how come I make $40,000 a year and you make $1,500,000 when you and I are doing basically the same work?"

The cardiologist paused, leaned over, and then whispered to the mechanic, "Try doing it with the engine running."

257.

A man is out driving in his Lada when it breaks down on the autobahn. Soon afterwards a Porsche pulls up behind the Lada.

"Do you want a tow?" asked the Porsche driver.

"Yes please, thank you," exclaimed the Lada driver, "I will put on my indicators if I think you are going too fast."

The Porsche driver agrees and sets off towing the Lada, After about half an hour a Lamborghini comes alongside the Porsche and challenges the driver to a race. Forgetting all about the Lada the Porsche driver accepts the challenge and the two of them fly down the autobahn at top speed

About 5km later a man is sitting by himself outside of a roadside pub and sees the three cars flying by. He rushes back into the pub and exclaims to his friends: "You will NEVER guess what I just saw"

"What?" Ask the man's friends eager to find out what he saw.

"I just saw a Porsche and a Lamborghini racing down the autobahn and a Lada indicating to overtake".

258.

Many years ago, we were cruising around Cambridge with Ray Magliozzi from Car Talk.

We came up to a light that just turned red and instead of slowing down, Ray put his foot right to the floor. I yelled out "Ray, you're going to get us killed!"

Ray laughs and says, "Take it easy, man, Tommy drives like this."

We hit another red light and Ray blazes right through. "Seriously, we're gonna die!" I screamed.

"Relax, this is how Tommy drives."

Finally, we come to a green light. He stops dead and looks both ways.

"Ray, what are you doing?" I asked.

He looked at me and said, "Tommy might be coming the other way."

259.

Five Dutchmen crammed into an old Renault 4 are driving through Belgium when they get pulled over by the traffic police.

"Good morning, I guess you know why I pulled you guys over, don't you?"

"Well officer, I actually don't. We couldn't have been speeding, this car won't even make the speed limit."

"No, no, it's not that. Do you not realize what car you're driving?"

"Yes sir, a classic Renault 4"

"Right. And how many of you are in the car?"

"Five, sir."

"There you go. One too many. Renault 4 is for four people." The driver looks at the cop, slightly baffled.

"Sir, the number 4 doesn't mean only four people are allowed to ride. I know it's a bit cramped, but surely not illegal."

"Are you telling me I don't know the rules?" the cop says angrily.

"No, no, not at all sir, it's just. Renault 4 is just the model number, not the capacity." The cop, looking a bit unsure now, scratches his head and says "Alright, I'll call my boss to check." (On the radio) "Boss, Stef here, listen ... I've got five Hollanders here in a Renault 4 and they insist this isn't illegal."

"Stef, I don't have time for your stupid questions right now. I've got three Italians in a Fiat Uno here!"

260.

A man walked out to the street and caught a taxi just going by. He got into the taxi, and the cabbie said, "Perfect timing. You're just like Ryan"

Passenger: "Who?"

Cabbie: "Ryan Jay Robinson. He's a guy who did everything right all the time. Like my coming along when you needed a cab, things happen like that to Ryan Jay Robinson, every single time."

Passenger: "There are always a few clouds over everybody."

Cabbie: "Not Ryan Jay Robinson. He was a terrific athlete. He could have won the Grand Slam at tennis. He could golf with the pros. He sang like an opera baritone and danced like a Broadway star, and you should have heard him play the piano. He was an amazing guy."

Passenger: "Sounds like he was something really special."

Cabbie: "There's more. He had a memory like a computer. He remembered everybody's birthday. He knew all about wine, which foods to order and which fork to eat them with. He could fix anything. Not like me. I change a fuse, and the whole street blacks out. But Ryan Jay Robinson, he could do everything right."

Passenger: "Wow. Some guy then."

Cabbie: "He always knew the quickest way to go in traffic and avoid traffic jams. Not like me, I always seem to get stuck in them. But Ryan, he never made a mistake, and he really knew how to treat a woman and make her feel good. He would never answer her back even if she was in the wrong; and his clothing was always immaculate, shoes highly polished too. He was the perfect man! He never made a mistake. No one could ever measure up to Ryan Jay Robinson."

Passenger: "An amazing fellow. How did you meet him?"

Cabbie: "Well, I never actually met Ryan. He died. I'm going to marry his widow next week."

261.

Husband: My wife is missing. She went to rescue people from the flood yesterday and has not returned home since.

Sergeant at the police station: What's her height?

Husband: Gee, I'm not sure. A little over five feet tall?

Sergeant: Weight?

Husband: Don't know. Not slim, not fat either.

Sergeant: Color of eyes?

Husband: Sort of brown, I think. I don't actually know. I've never even noticed.

Sergeant: What was she wearing?

Husband: Could have been pants, or maybe a skirt or shorts. I don't know exactly.

Sergeant: What kind of car did she go in?

Husband: She went in my Jeep.

Sergeant: What kind of Jeep was it?

Husband: It's a 2010 Rubicon with Sprintex Supercharger with Intercooler, DiabloSport T-1000 Trinity Programmer, Teraflex Falcon 3.3 Shocks, 1350

RE Reel Drive Shafts, Method 105 Bead Locks, Toyo 37" X 13.5" Tires, Custom Olympic Off Road Front Bumper, Olympic Off Road Smuggler Rear Bumper with a tire carrier, Seward Radius 4s LED light, Seward 12" LED light bar, 50" LED light bar with sPod LED switch pod with Boost gage, Rigid LED lights, 15 V Power Tank, Rock Hard Cage, Rock Hard Under Armor, Posion Spyder Extreme Duty Trans-Mount Cross Member, Buchwacker rear armor, 5.13 Gears, Magnum 44 Front Axle, Off Road Evolution "C" Gussets, Cobra 75 CB Radio, warn 10K on front and 8K winch on rear, Bartact seat covers, Delta Quad bar xenon headlamps, Tantrum LED offroad rock lights, Teraflex HD tie rod, Teraflex Falcon Steering stabilizer, Teraflex alpine long control arms front and rear, Teraflex 4" springs, Teraflex JK Performance slotted big rotor kit, Teraflex Monster HD forged front adjustable trackbar, Teraflex front and rear brake line kit, Teraflex bump stops front and rear, surprise straps, hothead headliner, Teraflex D-44 diff covers, Wild Boar grille, Rigid Ridge hood, Drake hood latch's and a Tuffy Security drawer.

Sergeant: Don't worry buddy. We'll find your Jeep.

262.

A man walked out to the street and caught a taxi just going by. He got into the taxi, and the cabbie said, "Perfect timing. You're just like Ryan"

Passenger: "Who?"

Cabbie: "Ryan Jay Robinson. He's a guy who did everything right all the time. Like my coming along when you needed a cab, things happen like that to Ryan Jay Robinson, every single time."

Passenger: "There are always a few clouds over everybody."

Cabbie: "Not Ryan Jay Robinson. He was a terrific athlete. He could have won the Grand Slam at tennis. He could golf with the pros. He sang like an opera baritone and danced like a Broadway star, and you should have heard him play the piano. He was an amazing guy."

Passenger: "Sounds like he was something really special."

Cabbie: "There's more. He had a memory like a computer. He remembered everybody's birthday. He knew all about wine, which foods to order and which fork to eat them with. He could fix anything. Not like me. I change a fuse, and the whole street blacks out. But Ryan Jay Robinson, he could do everything right."

Passenger: "Wow. Some guy then."

Cabbie: "He always knew the quickest way to go in traffic and avoid traffic jams. Not like me, I always seem to get stuck in them. But Ryan, he never made a mistake, and he really knew how to treat a woman and make her feel good. He would never answer her back even if she was in the wrong; and his clothing was always immaculate, shoes highly polished too. He was the perfect man! He never made a mistake. No one could ever measure up to Ryan Jay Robinson."

Passenger: "An amazing fellow. How did you meet him?"

Cabbie: "Well, I never actually met Ryan. He died. I'm going to marry his widow next week."

263.

Three men are waiting in line to address St Peter at the pearly gates.

St Peter asks the first man, "Were you faithful in your marriage?"

The 1st man replies, "I guess I can't lie here, so yes. Yes, I did many times."

Peter replies, "For all eternity this rusted out Volkswagen shall be your means of transportation," and continues with a "Next!"

Peter asks the same question to the 2nd man to which the man answers, "I did only once, and I still regret it."

St Peter: "Right! Toyota Corolla, No AC and no radio. Next!"

The third man proudly boasted that he was always faithful.

St Peter says. "Yes, we know, and you shall have this solid gold Cadillac to enjoy for all eternity. Off you go then"

One year later the Volkswagen man sees the Cadillac man and pulls over to say hello but finds the man crying intensely over the steering wheel.

"Hey Mr. Faithful, what could be so bad? We're in

Heaven and all's good right?"

The man replies, "You don't understand. My wife just arrived today!"

"That's great buddy! Together for eternity. So why the waterworks?" says the Volkswagen man.

The Cadillac man screams, "SHE WAS DRIVING A DACIA!"

264.

A father comes home and asks where his son is. His wife replies that he's downstairs playing with his new chemistry set.

The father is curious, so he wanders downstairs to see what his son is doing. As he's walking down the steps, he hears a banging sound. When he gets to the bottom, he sees his son pounding a nail into the wall.

He says to his son, "What are you doing? I thought you were playing with your chemistry set. Why are you hammering a nail into the wall?"

His son replies, "This isn't a nail, dad, it's a worm. I put these chemicals on it, and it became hard as a rock."

His dad thought about it for a minute and said, "I'll tell you what son, give me those chemicals and I'll give you a new Volkswagen."

His son quite naturally said, "Sure, why not."

The next day his son went into the garage to see his new car. Parked in the garage was a brand-new Mercedes.

Just then his dad walked in. He asked his father where his Volkswagen was.

"It's right there behind the Mercedes," replied the father,

"The Mercedes is from your mother."

265.

Three soldiers, one English, one French and one German, are captured by the Taliban in Afghanistan. Their captors take them to a mine field and tell them that if they can escape to the checkpoint on the other side, they are free to go. To do so they offer them each whatever transport they want to cross it.

The Englishman chooses a Rover, solidly built enough to take a blow from a mine perhaps. He hits a mine and explodes. Dead.

The Frenchman chooses a Renault, small and quick so it may be able to get between the mines, he thinks. He hits a mine and explodes. Dead.

The German asks for a large rubber duck, with a spring stuck on each corner. The Taliban suspect him to be mad, but its good sport so they find him a big rubber duck and kit it out as per his instructions.

He bounces his contraption over the mine field. He hits a mine and explodes. But the explosion carries him forward and he bounces to the next one. He crosses the whole minefield unharmed.

The Taliban at the other side is perplexed by this. "How did you ever manage to devise such a solution to crossing minefields?" they ask.

"Oh, it is an old German method," he replies, "We call it the Four-Sprung Duck Technique."

266.

A guy buys a new Peugeot and takes his 3 friends out for a ride. He's going fast, over the speed limit, violently hitting speed bumps.

First guy says: "Hey man, you're going a bit fast, slow down a bit"

Driver: "Are you an expert in Peugeot?"

Guy: "No"

Driver: "Then sit down and be quite"

Driver keeps speeding, zigzagging between cars at crazy speeds.

Second guy: "Slow down, you're driving too dangerously!"

Driver replies: "Are you an expert in Peugeot?"

Guy: "No"

Driver: "Then sit down and be quite"

Now the driver is way over the speed limit, running red lights and almost hitting an old lady. He's visibly losing control.

Third guy: "SLOW DOWN YOU'RE GONNA KILL

US ALL!"

Driver: "ARE YOU AN EXPERT IN PEUGEOT?"

Guy: "YES, YES I AM!"

Driver: "THEN TELL ME HOW TO STOP IT"

267.

A blonde enters a bank in New York City and asks for the Loan officer. She says she's going to Europe on business for two weeks and needs to borrow $ 5,000.

The bank officer says the bank will need some kind of security for the loan so the blond hands over the keys to a new Mercedes Benz SL 500.

The car is parked on the street in front of the bank. She has the title, and everything checks out and the bank agrees to accept the car collateral for the loan.

The bank's president and its officers all enjoy a good laugh at the blond for using a $110,000 Benz as collateral against a $5,000 loan.

An employee of the bank then proceeds to drive the Benz into the bank's underground garage and parks it there. Two weeks later, the blond returns and pays back the $5,000 and the interest which was at $15,41.

The loan officer says: Miss, we are happy to have had your business and this transaction has worked out nicely. But we are a little puzzled. While you were away, we checked you out and found that you are a multimillionaire. What puzzles us is, why would you bother to borrow $5,000?

The blond replies: Where else in New York City can I

park my car for two weeks for only $15.41 and expect it to be there when I return?

268.

A car collector from New York finally gets the Datsun he's been looking for.

Unfortunately, it was missing a few key parts to get it up and running. He takes it to his mechanic. The mechanic says "you need some specific gear parts here - these cogs over here, you'll need two of them. You can only get them from this specialty parts dealer, and he's in California.

The man decides to make a trip of it and goes out west. He finds the dealer and decides to buy a whole case of the parts and give the extras to his mechanic, maybe help out the next collector.

As they are flying home the following week, the pilot comes on over the speaker and says that they are having engine trouble and they will have to dump some cargo to stay in the air.

The man says that he has a very heavy box of car parts in Cargo and asks if they can just take two of the parts out and dump the rest.

Meanwhile, somewhere in the mid-west in the middle of the night a farmer and his wife start hearing Bang! Bang! as stuff from the plane is landing all around them and on their roof.

The farmer's wife looks out the window and says "You won't believe it; it's raining Datsun cogs"

269.

How do you kill a blue Elephant?

With a blue elephant gun obviously.

How do you kill a red elephant?

You choke it till it turns blue then use a blue elephant gun.

How do you kill a green elephant?

You tickle it till it turns red then choke it till it turns blue then use a blue elephant gun.

How do you kill a purple elephant?

There's no such thing as a purple elephant you moron.

How many elephants will fit in a Volkswagen?

Four, two in the front and two in the back.

How do you know if there's an elephant in your refrigerator?

Elephant tracks in the butter.

How do you know if there's two elephants in your refrigerator?

Two sets of tracks.

How do you know if there's three elephants in your refrigerator?

The door won't close.

How do you know if there's four elephants in your refrigerator?

There's a Volkswagen parked out front.

Dear reader

Thank you for purchasing this book. I hope you have had as much joy reading it as I have had making it. If you liked it, please consider giving it an honest review on Amazon. It would be very much appreciated and a great help in my book publishing journey.

If you want more similar jokes sent to you then don't hesitate to use the funnel on page 5 where you can access the free **Motorcycle Jokes** book.

Stay safe on the road,

Hugh Phunnie.

HUGH PHUNNIE

Books by the Author

Bad Dad Jokes: *450 Chringeworthy and Silly Dad Jokes for All the Family.*

Halloween Joke Book for Kids: *250 Horribly Funny Jokes for All the Family.*

The Automobile Joke Book: *The #1 Joke Book for All Car Enthusiasts and Petrolheads!*

Would You Rather? Christmas Edition: *A Fun Christmas Holiday Themed Activity Book for All the Family and Kids.*

HUGH PHUNNIE

THE AUTOMOBILE JOKE BOOK

Published by

Rittin Books ©

Printed in Great Britain
by Amazon